Dedication:

💗 For my wonderful, supportive family, especially my daughters BethAnn and Laura, and my grandchildren Isabella and Ryan, you are the inspiration for my work to help children and adults diagnosed with brain disorders to live their best lives.

💗 For every child and adult who lives daily with the challenges of sensory processing disorder or any brain disorder, and for those who love them, I dedicate this book to you.

A special thank you to my amazing husband Jim, who has always been there to support me!

And thank you Nejla Shojaie for your beautiful illustrations, as you truly brought my book to life!

ISBN: 979-8-9906463-0-8

The Bumps On My Socks

and Other Things That Bother My Brain

Written by
Colleen Russell

Illustrated by
Nejla Shojaie

The bumps on my socks I feel on my feet,
but they bother my brain too.

I can't think of anything else but those bumps
and I don't know what to do.

The tag on my shirt and sweaters that itch
do the same thing to me.

They scratch and itch and itch and scratch
and make me feel grumpy.

When lights are too bright and noises too loud, these really give me a scare.

Thunderstorms are the worst of all,
and no one else seems to care.

Doors that slam and balloons that pop make me cover my head.

When people yell and scream too much
I want to hide under my bed.

I worry a lot about everything,
and I don't even know why.

What if Mommy and Daddy are not okay?
My thoughts make me want to cry.

At night when I sleep
I can have scary dreams.

When do the bad dreams end?
Am I awake,
or am I still sleeping?
I can't tell the real from pretend.

Please don't make fun, or yell at me.
I don't mean to make you mad.

I feel that I can't do anything right,
and that makes me very sad.

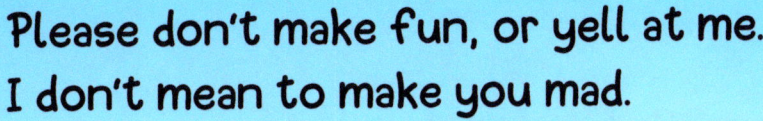

Instead, help me make my brain work better, and here are some things you can do.

Know that certain things are hard for me that may seem easy for you.

Sometimes I need the lights turned down low, and noises to not be so loud.

Some places are hard for me to be in,
especially ones with big crowds.

My headphones can help
to keep me calm, and quiet
the bothersome sounds.

Let me have a safe place where I can go with no one else around.

Give me extra time to finish my chores.

I do better when not in a hurry.

Help me stay on task one step at a time
and remind me not to worry.

Hold me close and tell me I'm safe
when I wake from a scary dream.

Let me sit with you and take slow deep
breaths so it won't be as bad as it seems.

Tell me when I am being good.
I don't want to think I am bad.

My tummy feels so much better inside
when I am happy instead of sad.

Help me pick the right clothes that won't make me itch or ones that don't give me a pain.

Let me fix my socks or take them off when the bumps bother my brain.

What are some things that bother your brain?

1.

2.

3.

4.

5.

What are some things that can help your brain to work better?

1.

2.

3.

4.

5.

Meet The Author:

Mary "Colleen" Daniels Russell is a wife, mother, grandmother and recently retired nurse. Colleen has a Bachelor's Degree from the University of Delaware and a Master's Degree from Duke University. She has spent more than 40 years working with children in a variety of clinical settings, and several years as a psychiatric nursing instructor. Colleen's greatest passion is caring for people with mental illness and educating them and their families. Her goal with this book is to help children with sensory processing disorder and all who care for them.

Meet The Illustrator:

Nejla Shojaie is an illustrator. She has loved to draw since she was a child. She loves working and living her life as an illustrator and creating children's illustrations. She likes traveling, reading, watching movies and enjoys listening to music, especially when she's drawing.

www.ingramcontent.com/pod-product-compliance
Lightning Source LLC
Chambersburg PA
CBHW041501120626
46547CB00003B/501